Practicing Numbers
1–100

Name

To parents/guardia
1–100. If they are having difficulty with this section, try some extended practice with numbers before continuing.

■ Say each number aloud as you write it.

1	2	3	4	5	6	7	8	9	10

11	12	13	14	15	16	17	18	19	20

21	22	23	24	25	26	27	28	29	30

31	32	33	34	35	36	37	38	39	40

41	42	43	44	45	46	47	48	49	50

■ Say each number aloud as you write it.

51	52	53	54	55	56	57	58	59	60
51									

61	62	63	64	65	66	67	68	69	70

71	72	73	74	75	76	77	78	79	80

81	82	83	84	85	86	87	88	89	90

91	92	93	94	95	96	97	98	99	100

Review
Multiplication 1 and 2

Name

Date
/ /

To parents/guardians: Your child will review multiplication from one to five. If your child encounters difficulty during this review, perhaps some extended review with "My Book of Simple Multiplication" would be a good idea.

■ Multiply.

(1) $1 \times 1 =$

(2) $1 \times 2 =$

(3) $1 \times 3 =$

(4) $1 \times 4 =$

(5) $1 \times 5 =$

(6) $1 \times 6 =$

(7) $1 \times 7 =$

(8) $1 \times 8 =$

(9) $1 \times 9 =$

(10) $1 \times 10 =$

(11) $2 \times 1 =$

(12) $2 \times 2 =$

(13) $2 \times 3 =$

(14) $2 \times 4 =$

(15) $2 \times 5 =$

(16) $2 \times 6 =$

(17) $2 \times 7 =$

(18) $2 \times 8 =$

(19) $2 \times 9 =$

(20) $2 \times 10 =$

■ Multiply.

(1) $1 \times 9 =$

(2) $1 \times 7 =$

(3) $1 \times 5 =$

(4) $1 \times 1 =$

(5) $1 \times 4 =$

(6) $1 \times 8 =$

(7) $1 \times 6 =$

(8) $1 \times 3 =$

(9) $1 \times 10 =$

(10) $1 \times 2 =$

(11) $2 \times 3 =$

(12) $2 \times 8 =$

(13) $2 \times 9 =$

(14) $2 \times 10 =$

(15) $2 \times 2 =$

(16) $2 \times 4 =$

(17) $2 \times 6 =$

(18) $2 \times 7 =$

(19) $2 \times 5 =$

(20) $2 \times 1 =$

3 Review
Multiplication 3 and 4

Name

Date
/ /

■ Multiply.

(1) $3 \times 1 =$

(2) $3 \times 2 =$

(3) $3 \times 3 =$

(4) $3 \times 4 =$

(5) $3 \times 5 =$

(6) $3 \times 6 =$

(7) $3 \times 7 =$

(8) $3 \times 8 =$

(9) $3 \times 9 =$

(10) $3 \times 10 =$

(11) $4 \times 1 =$

(12) $4 \times 2 =$

(13) $4 \times 3 =$

(14) $4 \times 4 =$

(15) $4 \times 5 =$

(16) $4 \times 6 =$

(17) $4 \times 7 =$

(18) $4 \times 8 =$

(19) $4 \times 9 =$

(20) $4 \times 10 =$

■Multiply.

(1) $3 \times 3 =$

(2) $3 \times 7 =$

(3) $3 \times 9 =$

(4) $3 \times 1 =$

(5) $3 \times 2 =$

(6) $3 \times 10 =$

(7) $3 \times 6 =$

(8) $3 \times 4 =$

(9) $3 \times 5 =$

(10) $3 \times 8 =$

(11) $4 \times 7 =$

(12) $4 \times 8 =$

(13) $4 \times 1 =$

(14) $4 \times 9 =$

(15) $4 \times 5 =$

(16) $4 \times 10 =$

(17) $4 \times 4 =$

(18) $4 \times 6 =$

(19) $4 \times 2 =$

(20) $4 \times 3 =$

Review
Multiplication 1 to 5

■ Multiply.

(1) 5 × 1 =

(2) 5 × 2 =

(3) 5 × 3 =

(4) 5 × 4 =

(5) 5 × 5 =

(6) 5 × 6 =

(7) 5 × 7 =

(8) 5 × 8 =

(9) 5 × 9 =

(10) 5 × 10 =

(11) 1 × 2 =

(12) 1 × 6 =

(13) 1 × 7 =

(14) 1 × 10 =

(15) 2 × 1 =

(16) 2 × 4 =

(17) 2 × 8 =

(18) 2 × 9 =

(19) 3 × 3 =

(20) 3 × 5 =

■Multiply.

(1) $3 \times 6 =$

(2) $3 \times 10 =$

(3) $4 \times 2 =$

(4) $4 \times 4 =$

(5) $4 \times 5 =$

(6) $4 \times 8 =$

(7) $5 \times 1 =$

(8) $5 \times 3 =$

(9) $5 \times 7 =$

(10) $5 \times 9 =$

(11) $1 \times 3 =$

(12) $1 \times 9 =$

(13) $2 \times 2 =$

(14) $2 \times 10 =$

(15) $3 \times 5 =$

(16) $3 \times 8 =$

(17) $4 \times 1 =$

(18) $4 \times 7 =$

(19) $5 \times 4 =$

(20) $5 \times 6 =$

5 Review
Multiplication 1 to 5

■ Multiply.

(1) $1 \times 3 =$

(2) $2 \times 1 =$

(3) $3 \times 4 =$

(4) $4 \times 5 =$

(5) $5 \times 2 =$

(6) $1 \times 6 =$

(7) $2 \times 8 =$

(8) $3 \times 10 =$

(9) $4 \times 9 =$

(10) $5 \times 7 =$

(11) $1 \times 8 =$

(12) $2 \times 10 =$

(13) $3 \times 6 =$

(14) $4 \times 7 =$

(15) $5 \times 9 =$

(16) $1 \times 1 =$

(17) $2 \times 4 =$

(18) $3 \times 5 =$

(19) $4 \times 2 =$

(20) $5 \times 3 =$

■Multiply.

(1) $2 \times 4 =$

(2) $1 \times 7 =$

(3) $4 \times 2 =$

(4) $5 \times 8 =$

(5) $3 \times 10 =$

(6) $5 \times 1 =$

(7) $4 \times 9 =$

(8) $3 \times 6 =$

(9) $1 \times 3 =$

(10) $2 \times 5 =$

(11) $4 \times 6 =$

(12) $2 \times 10 =$

(13) $5 \times 5 =$

(14) $1 \times 1 =$

(15) $3 \times 8 =$

(16) $2 \times 2 =$

(17) $5 \times 3 =$

(18) $4 \times 7 =$

(19) $3 \times 9 =$

(20) $1 \times 4 =$

Name

Date / /

To parents/guardians: The aim of this unit is to expose your child to the concept of multiplication in a fun way. In activities such as drawing lines or tracing numbers in a number chart, your child should say the numbers out loud as they proceed.

■ Draw a line from 6 to 60 in order while saying each number aloud.

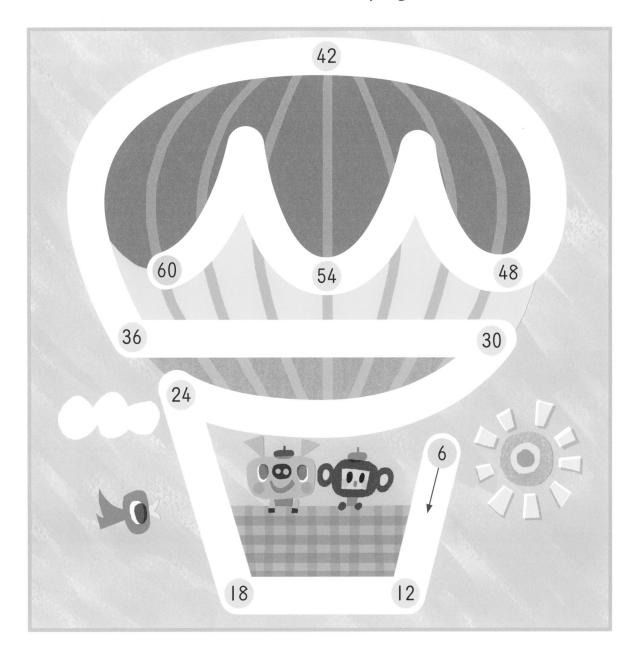

■ Say each number aloud as you trace it.

| 6 | 12 | 18 | 24 | 30 | 36 | 42 | 48 | 54 | 60 |

■ Add.

(1) 6 + 6 = 12

(2) 6 + 6 + 6 = 18

(3) 6 + 6 + 6 + 6 = 24

(4) 6 + 6 + 6 + 6 + 6 = 30

(5) 6 + 6 + 6 + 6 + 6 + 6 = 36

(6) 6 + 6 + 6 + 6 + 6 + 6 + 6 = 42

(7) 6 + 6 + 6 + 6 + 6 + 6 + 6 + 6 = 48

(8) 6 + 6 + 6 + 6 + 6 + 6 + 6 + 6 + 6 = 54

(9) 6 + 6 + 6 + 6 + 6 + 6 + 6 + 6 + 6 + 6 = 60

■ Say each number aloud as you trace it.

| 6 | 12 | 18 | 24 | 30 | 36 | 42 | 48 | 54 | 60 |

Practicing Repeated Addition

6–60

Name

Date

/   /

To parents/guardians: Repeated addition is good preparation for multiplication. In order to help your child see the link between multiplication and repeated addition, ask them how many sixes there are in the number sentences below.

■ Say each number aloud as you trace it.

| 6 | 12 | 18 | 24 | 30 |

(1) $6 + 6 = 12$

(2) $6 + 6 + 6 = 18$

(3) $6 + 6 + 6 + 6 = 24$

(4) $6 + 6 + 6 + 6 + 6 = 30$

■ Write the numbers on the number line. Then add the numbers below.

| 6 | | | | |

(1) $6 + 6 =$

(2) $6 + 6 + 6 =$

(3) $6 + 6 + 6 + 6 =$

(4) $6 + 6 + 6 + 6 + 6 =$

■ Say each number aloud as you trace it.

36	42	48	54	60

(1) $6 + 6 + 6 + 6 + 6 + 6 = 36$

(2) $6 + 6 + 6 + 6 + 6 + 6 + 6 = 42$

(3) $6 + 6 + 6 + 6 + 6 + 6 + 6 + 6 = 48$

(4) $6 + 6 + 6 + 6 + 6 + 6 + 6 + 6 + 6 = 54$

(5) $6 + 6 + 6 + 6 + 6 + 6 + 6 + 6 + 6 + 6 = 60$

■ Write the numbers on the number line. Then add the numbers below.

36				

(1) $6 + 6 + 6 + 6 + 6 + 6 =$

(2) $6 + 6 + 6 + 6 + 6 + 6 + 6 =$

(3) $6 + 6 + 6 + 6 + 6 + 6 + 6 + 6 =$

(4) $6 + 6 + 6 + 6 + 6 + 6 + 6 + 6 + 6 =$

(5) $6 + 6 + 6 + 6 + 6 + 6 + 6 + 6 + 6 + 6 =$

8 Multiplication 6
6 × 1 to 6 × 10

Name

Date / /

To parents/guardians: Starting on this page, your child will practice the multiplication table for the number 6. If your child has difficulty understanding these number sentences, help them understand that 6 × 3 is "three groups of six."

■ Read the multiplication table aloud.

Multiplication Table

(1) $6 \times 1 = 6$	Six times one is six.
(2) $6 \times 2 = 12$	Six times two is twelve.
(3) $6 \times 3 = 18$	Six times three is eighteen.
(4) $6 \times 4 = 24$	Six times four is twenty-four.
(5) $6 \times 5 = 30$	Six times five is thirty.
(6) $6 \times 6 = 36$	Six times six is thirty-six.
(7) $6 \times 7 = 42$	Six times seven is forty-two.
(8) $6 \times 8 = 48$	Six times eight is forty-eight.
(9) $6 \times 9 = 54$	Six times nine is fifty-four.
(10) $6 \times 10 = 60$	Six times ten is sixty.

■ Read each number sentence aloud as you trace the answer.

(1) $6 \times 1 = 6$

(2) $6 \times 2 = 12$

(3) $6 \times 3 = 18$

(4) $6 \times 4 = 24$

(5) $6 \times 5 = 30$

(6) $6 \times 6 = 36$

(7) $6 \times 7 = 42$

(8) $6 \times 8 = 48$

(9) $6 \times 9 = 54$

(10) $6 \times 10 = 60$

■ Multiply.

(1) $6 \times 1 =$

(2) $6 \times 2 =$

(3) $6 \times 3 =$

(4) $6 \times 4 =$

(5) $6 \times 5 =$

(6) $6 \times 6 =$

(7) $6 \times 7 =$

(8) $6 \times 8 =$

(9) $6 \times 9 =$

(10) $6 \times 10 =$

(11) $6 \times 1 =$

(12) $6 \times 2 =$

(13) $6 \times 3 =$

(14) $6 \times 4 =$

(15) $6 \times 5 =$

(16) $6 \times 6 =$

(17) $6 \times 7 =$

(18) $6 \times 8 =$

(19) $6 \times 9 =$

(20) $6 \times 10 =$

Multiplication 6
6 × 1 to 6 × 10

To parents/guardians: If your child has difficulty answering the multiplication problems below, they can go back to the previous page and review the Multiplication Table. It is a good idea to have your child review the Multiplication Table repeatedly.

■ Multiply.

(1) 6 × 3 =

(2) 6 × 6 =

(3) 6 × 9 =

(4) 6 × 5 =

(5) 6 × 1 =

(6) 6 × 7 =

(7) 6 × 2 =

(8) 6 × 8 =

(9) 6 × 10 =

(10) 6 × 4 =

(11) 6 × 9 =

(12) 6 × 1 =

(13) 6 × 7 =

(14) 6 × 10 =

(15) 6 × 8 =

(16) 6 × 3 =

(17) 6 × 5 =

(18) 6 × 2 =

(19) 6 × 4 =

(20) 6 × 6 =

■Multiply.

(1) $6 \times 4 =$

(2) $6 \times 7 =$

(3) $6 \times 10 =$

(4) $6 \times 2 =$

(5) $6 \times 6 =$

(6) $6 \times 1 =$

(7) $6 \times 8 =$

(8) $6 \times 3 =$

(9) $6 \times 9 =$

(10) $6 \times 5 =$

(11) $6 \times 9 =$

(12) $6 \times 3 =$

(13) $6 \times 1 =$

(14) $6 \times 4 =$

(15) $6 \times 10 =$

(16) $6 \times 5 =$

(17) $6 \times 7 =$

(18) $6 \times 2 =$

(19) $6 \times 8 =$

(20) $6 \times 6 =$

Multiplication 6
6 × 1 to 6 × 10

To parents/guardians: It takes a lot of concentration for your child to practice 40 multiplication problems in one sitting. If your child has trouble concentrating, it is okay for them to take a break.

■ Multiply.

(1) 6 × 7 =

(2) 6 × 3 =

(3) 6 × 6 =

(4) 6 × 1 =

(5) 6 × 10 =

(6) 6 × 5 =

(7) 6 × 9 =

(8) 6 × 4 =

(9) 6 × 2 =

(10) 6 × 8 =

(11) 6 × 2 =

(12) 6 × 5 =

(13) 6 × 9 =

(14) 6 × 7 =

(15) 6 × 3 =

(16) 6 × 1 =

(17) 6 × 8 =

(18) 6 × 6 =

(19) 6 × 4 =

(20) 6 × 10 =

■ Multiply.

(1) 6 × 1 =

(2) 6 × 8 =

(3) 6 × 10 =

(4) 6 × 3 =

(5) 6 × 6 =

(6) 6 × 2 =

(7) 6 × 7 =

(8) 6 × 4 =

(9) 6 × 5 =

(10) 6 × 9 =

(11) 6 × 4 =

(12) 6 × 9 =

(13) 6 × 1 =

(14) 6 × 5 =

(15) 6 × 10 =

(16) 6 × 6 =

(17) 6 × 2 =

(18) 6 × 8 =

(19) 6 × 3 =

(20) 6 × 7 =

Practicing Numbers
7–70

Name

Date

/ /

To parents/guardians: You may want to encourage your child to repeat the number that increases by 7 while looking at a number chart or addition problem.

■ Draw a line from 7 to 70 in order while saying each number aloud.

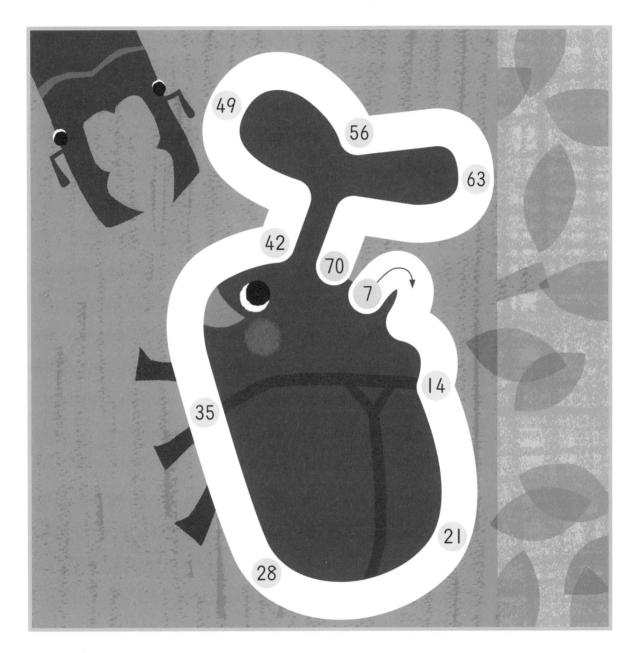

■ Say each number aloud as you trace it.

7	14	21	28	35	42	49	56	63	70

■ Add.

(1) $7 + 7 = 14$

(2) $7 + 7 + 7 = 21$

(3) $7 + 7 + 7 + 7 = 28$

(4) $7 + 7 + 7 + 7 + 7 = 35$

(5) $7 + 7 + 7 + 7 + 7 + 7 = 42$

(6) $7 + 7 + 7 + 7 + 7 + 7 + 7 = 49$

(7) $7 + 7 + 7 + 7 + 7 + 7 + 7 + 7 = 56$

(8) $7 + 7 + 7 + 7 + 7 + 7 + 7 + 7 + 7 = 63$

(9) $7 + 7 + 7 + 7 + 7 + 7 + 7 + 7 + 7 + 7 = 70$

■ Say each number aloud as you trace it.

| 7 | 14 | 21 | 28 | 35 | 42 | 49 | 56 | 63 | 70 |

Practicing Repeated Addition

7–70

To parents/guardians: Repeated addition is good preparation for multiplication. In order to help your child see the link between multiplication and repeated addition, ask them how many sevens there are in the number sentences below.

■ Say each number aloud as you trace it.

7	14	21	28	35

(1) $7 + 7 = 14$

(2) $7 + 7 + 7 = 21$

(3) $7 + 7 + 7 + 7 = 28$

(4) $7 + 7 + 7 + 7 + 7 = 35$

■ Write the numbers on the number line. Then add the numbers below.

7				

(1) $7 + 7 =$

(2) $7 + 7 + 7 =$

(3) $7 + 7 + 7 + 7 =$

(4) $7 + 7 + 7 + 7 + 7 =$

■ Say each number aloud as you trace it.

42	49	56	63	70

(1) $7 + 7 + 7 + 7 + 7 + 7 = 42$

(2) $7 + 7 + 7 + 7 + 7 + 7 + 7 = 49$

(3) $7 + 7 + 7 + 7 + 7 + 7 + 7 + 7 = 56$

(4) $7 + 7 + 7 + 7 + 7 + 7 + 7 + 7 + 7 = 63$

(5) $7 + 7 + 7 + 7 + 7 + 7 + 7 + 7 + 7 + 7 = 70$

■ Write the numbers on the number line. Then add the numbers below.

42				

(1) $7 + 7 + 7 + 7 + 7 + 7 =$

(2) $7 + 7 + 7 + 7 + 7 + 7 + 7 =$

(3) $7 + 7 + 7 + 7 + 7 + 7 + 7 + 7 =$

(4) $7 + 7 + 7 + 7 + 7 + 7 + 7 + 7 + 7 =$

(5) $7 + 7 + 7 + 7 + 7 + 7 + 7 + 7 + 7 + 7 =$

Multiplication 7
7 × 1 to 7 × 10

Name

Date

/ /

To parents/guardians: Starting on this page, your child will practice the multiplication table for the number 7. Give your child lots of praise when they can read each number sentence well.

■ Read the multiplication table aloud.

Multiplication Table

(1)	7	×	1	=	7	**Seven times one is seven.**
(2)	7	×	2	=	14	**Seven times two is fourteen.**
(3)	7	×	3	=	21	**Seven times three is twenty-one.**
(4)	7	×	4	=	28	**Seven times four is twenty-eight.**
(5)	7	×	5	=	35	**Seven times five is thirty-five.**
(6)	7	×	6	=	42	**Seven times six is forty-two.**
(7)	7	×	7	=	49	**Seven times seven is forty-nine.**
(8)	7	×	8	=	56	**Seven times eight is fifty-six.**
(9)	7	×	9	=	63	**Seven times nine is sixty-three.**
(10)	7	×	10	=	70	**Seven times ten is seventy.**

■ Read each number sentence aloud as you trace the answer.

(1) 7 × 1 = 7   (6) 7 × 6 = 42

(2) 7 × 2 = 14   (7) 7 × 7 = 49

(3) 7 × 3 = 21   (8) 7 × 8 = 56

(4) 7 × 4 = 28   (9) 7 × 9 = 63

(5) 7 × 5 = 35   (10) 7 × 10 = 70

7×6
7×7
7×8

■ Multiply.

(1) 7 × 1 =

(2) 7 × 2 =

(3) 7 × 3 =

(4) 7 × 4 =

(5) 7 × 5 =

(6) 7 × 6 =

(7) 7 × 7 =

(8) 7 × 8 =

(9) 7 × 9 =

(10) 7 × 10 =

(11) 7 × 1 =

(12) 7 × 2 =

(13) 7 × 3 =

(14) 7 × 4 =

(15) 7 × 5 =

(16) 7 × 6 =

(17) 7 × 7 =

(18) 7 × 8 =

(19) 7 × 9 =

(20) 7 × 10 =

Multiplication 7
7 × 1 to 7 × 10

To parents/guardians: If your child has difficulty with this section, you can have them to reread the Multiplication Table from the previous unit for help.

■ Multiply.

(1) $7 \times 3 =$

(2) $7 \times 6 =$

(3) $7 \times 9 =$

(4) $7 \times 5 =$

(5) $7 \times 1 =$

(6) $7 \times 7 =$

(7) $7 \times 2 =$

(8) $7 \times 8 =$

(9) $7 \times 10 =$

(10) $7 \times 4 =$

(11) $7 \times 9 =$

(12) $7 \times 1 =$

(13) $7 \times 7 =$

(14) $7 \times 10 =$

(15) $7 \times 8 =$

(16) $7 \times 3 =$

(17) $7 \times 5 =$

(18) $7 \times 2 =$

(19) $7 \times 4 =$

(20) $7 \times 6 =$

■ Multiply.

(1) $7 \times 4 =$

(2) $7 \times 7 =$

(3) $7 \times 10 =$

(4) $7 \times 2 =$

(5) $7 \times 6 =$

(6) $7 \times 1 =$

(7) $7 \times 8 =$

(8) $7 \times 3 =$

(9) $7 \times 9 =$

(10) $7 \times 5 =$

(11) $7 \times 9 =$

(12) $7 \times 3 =$

(13) $7 \times 1 =$

(14) $7 \times 4 =$

(15) $7 \times 10 =$

(16) $7 \times 5 =$

(17) $7 \times 7 =$

(18) $7 \times 2 =$

(19) $7 \times 8 =$

(20) $7 \times 6 =$

Multiplication 7
7 × 1 to 7 × 10

■ Multiply.

(1) $7 \times 7 =$

(2) $7 \times 3 =$

(3) $7 \times 6 =$

(4) $7 \times 1 =$

(5) $7 \times 10 =$

(6) $7 \times 5 =$

(7) $7 \times 9 =$

(8) $7 \times 4 =$

(9) $7 \times 2 =$

(10) $7 \times 8 =$

(11) $7 \times 2 =$

(12) $7 \times 5 =$

(13) $7 \times 9 =$

(14) $7 \times 7 =$

(15) $7 \times 3 =$

(16) $7 \times 1 =$

(17) $7 \times 8 =$

(18) $7 \times 6 =$

(19) $7 \times 4 =$

(20) $7 \times 10 =$

■Multiply.

(1) $7 \times 1 =$

(2) $7 \times 8 =$

(3) $7 \times 10 =$

(4) $7 \times 3 =$

(5) $7 \times 6 =$

(6) $7 \times 2 =$

(7) $7 \times 7 =$

(8) $7 \times 4 =$

(9) $7 \times 5 =$

(10) $7 \times 9 =$

(11) $7 \times 4 =$

(12) $7 \times 9 =$

(13) $7 \times 1 =$

(14) $7 \times 5 =$

(15) $7 \times 10 =$

(16) $7 \times 6 =$

(17) $7 \times 2 =$

(18) $7 \times 8 =$

(19) $7 \times 3 =$

(20) $7 \times 7 =$

Review
Multiplication 6, 7

To parents/guardians: Please confirm your child is able to write the correct answer. If your child can answer the problems correctly, offer lots of praise.

■ Multiply.

(1)　$6 \times 1 =$

(2)　$6 \times 2 =$

(3)　$6 \times 3 =$

(4)　$6 \times 4 =$

(5)　$6 \times 5 =$

(6)　$6 \times 6 =$

(7)　$6 \times 7 =$

(8)　$6 \times 8 =$

(9)　$6 \times 9 =$

(10)　$6 \times 10 =$

(11)　$7 \times 1 =$

(12)　$7 \times 2 =$

(13)　$7 \times 3 =$

(14)　$7 \times 4 =$

(15)　$7 \times 5 =$

(16)　$7 \times 6 =$

(17)　$7 \times 7 =$

(18)　$7 \times 8 =$

(19)　$7 \times 9 =$

(20)　$7 \times 10 =$

■ Multiply.

(1) $7 \times 9 =$

(2) $6 \times 7 =$

(3) $7 \times 5 =$

(4) $6 \times 6 =$

(5) $7 \times 1 =$

(6) $6 \times 8 =$

(7) $7 \times 10 =$

(8) $6 \times 3 =$

(9) $7 \times 2 =$

(10) $6 \times 4 =$

(11) $6 \times 10 =$

(12) $7 \times 3 =$

(13) $6 \times 1 =$

(14) $7 \times 8 =$

(15) $6 \times 5 =$

(16) $7 \times 6 =$

(17) $6 \times 2 =$

(18) $7 \times 4 =$

(19) $6 \times 9 =$

(20) $7 \times 7 =$

Practicing Numbers
8–80

To parents/guardians: When completing the following activities, your child should say the numbers aloud as they go.

■ Draw a line from 8 to 80 in order while saying each number aloud.

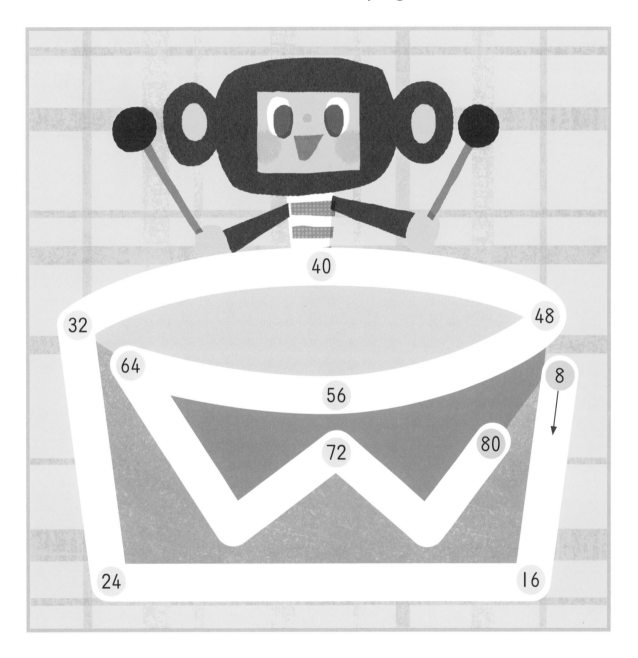

■ Say each number aloud as you trace it.

| 8 | 16 | 24 | 32 | 40 | 48 | 56 | 64 | 72 | 80 |

■ Add.

(1) $8 + 8 = 16$

(2) $8 + 8 + 8 = 24$

(3) $8 + 8 + 8 + 8 = 32$

(4) $8 + 8 + 8 + 8 + 8 = 40$

(5) $8 + 8 + 8 + 8 + 8 + 8 = 48$

(6) $8 + 8 + 8 + 8 + 8 + 8 + 8 = 56$

(7) $8 + 8 + 8 + 8 + 8 + 8 + 8 + 8 = 64$

(8) $8 + 8 + 8 + 8 + 8 + 8 + 8 + 8 + 8 = 72$

(9) $8 + 8 + 8 + 8 + 8 + 8 + 8 + 8 + 8 + 8 = 80$

■ Say each number aloud as you trace it.

8	16	24	32	40	48	56	64	72	80

Name

Date

/ /

■ Say each number aloud as you trace it.

| 8 | 16 | 24 | 32 | 40 |

(1) $8 + 8 = 16$

(2) $8 + 8 + 8 = 24$

(3) $8 + 8 + 8 + 8 = 32$

(4) $8 + 8 + 8 + 8 + 8 = 40$

■ Write the numbers on the number line. Then add the numbers below.

| 8 | | | |

(1) $8 + 8 =$

(2) $8 + 8 + 8 =$

(3) $8 + 8 + 8 + 8 =$

(4) $8 + 8 + 8 + 8 + 8 =$

■ Say each number aloud as you trace it.

48	56	64	72	80

(1) $8 + 8 + 8 + 8 + 8 + 8 = 48$

(2) $8 + 8 + 8 + 8 + 8 + 8 + 8 = 56$

(3) $8 + 8 + 8 + 8 + 8 + 8 + 8 + 8 = 64$

(4) $8 + 8 + 8 + 8 + 8 + 8 + 8 + 8 + 8 = 72$

(5) $8 + 8 + 8 + 8 + 8 + 8 + 8 + 8 + 8 + 8 = 80$

■ Write the numbers on the number line. Then add the numbers below.

48				

(1) $8 + 8 + 8 + 8 + 8 + 8 =$

(2) $8 + 8 + 8 + 8 + 8 + 8 + 8 =$

(3) $8 + 8 + 8 + 8 + 8 + 8 + 8 + 8 =$

(4) $8 + 8 + 8 + 8 + 8 + 8 + 8 + 8 + 8 =$

(5) $8 + 8 + 8 + 8 + 8 + 8 + 8 + 8 + 8 + 8 =$

Multiplication 8
8 × 1 to 8 × 10

To parents/guardians: Starting on this page, your child will practice the multiplication table for the number 8. If your child has difficulty understanding these number sentences, help them understand that 8 × 2 is "two groups of eight."

■ Read the multiplication table aloud.

Multiplication Table		
(1) $8 \times 1 = 8$	**Eight times one is eight.**	
(2) $8 \times 2 = 16$	**Eight times two is sixteen.**	
(3) $8 \times 3 = 24$	**Eight times three is twenty-four.**	
(4) $8 \times 4 = 32$	**Eight times four is thirty-two.**	
(5) $8 \times 5 = 40$	**Eight times five is forty.**	
(6) $8 \times 6 = 48$	**Eight times six is forty-eight.**	
(7) $8 \times 7 = 56$	**Eight times seven is fifty-six.**	
(8) $8 \times 8 = 64$	**Eight times eight is sixty-four.**	
(9) $8 \times 9 = 72$	**Eight times nine is seventy-two.**	
(10) $8 \times 10 = 80$	**Eight times ten is eighty.**	

■ Read each number sentence aloud as you trace the answer.

(1) $8 \times 1 = 8$

(2) $8 \times 2 = 16$

(3) $8 \times 3 = 24$

(4) $8 \times 4 = 32$

(5) $8 \times 5 = 40$

(6) $8 \times 6 = 48$

(7) $8 \times 7 = 56$

(8) $8 \times 8 = 64$

(9) $8 \times 9 = 72$

(10) $8 \times 10 = 80$

■ Multiply.

(1)　8　×　1　=

(2)　8　×　2　=

(3)　8　×　3　=

(4)　8　×　4　=

(5)　8　×　5　=

(6)　8　×　6　=

(7)　8　×　7　=

(8)　8　×　8　=

(9)　8　×　9　=

(10)　8　×　10　=

(11)　8　×　1　=

(12)　8　×　2　=

(13)　8　×　3　=

(14)　8　×　4　=

(15)　8　×　5　=

(16)　8　×　6　=

(17)　8　×　7　=

(18)　8　×　8　=

(19)　8　×　9　=

(20)　8　×　10　=

Name

Date / /

To parents/guardians: It takes a lot of concentration for your child to practice 40 multiplication problems in one sitting. If your child has trouble concentrating, it is okay for them to take a break.

■ Multiply.

(1) 8 × 3 =

(2) 8 × 6 =

(3) 8 × 9 =

(4) 8 × 5 =

(5) 8 × 1 =

(6) 8 × 7 =

(7) 8 × 2 =

(8) 8 × 8 =

(9) 8 × 10 =

(10) 8 × 4 =

(11) 8 × 9 =

(12) 8 × 1 =

(13) 8 × 7 =

(14) 8 × 10 =

(15) 8 × 8 =

(16) 8 × 3 =

(17) 8 × 5 =

(18) 8 × 2 =

(19) 8 × 4 =

(20) 8 × 6 =

■ Multiply.

(1) $8 \times 4 =$

(2) $8 \times 7 =$

(3) $8 \times 10 =$

(4) $8 \times 2 =$

(5) $8 \times 6 =$

(6) $8 \times 1 =$

(7) $8 \times 8 =$

(8) $8 \times 3 =$

(9) $8 \times 9 =$

(10) $8 \times 5 =$

(11) $8 \times 9 =$

(12) $8 \times 3 =$

(13) $8 \times 1 =$

(14) $8 \times 4 =$

(15) $8 \times 10 =$

(16) $8 \times 5 =$

(17) $8 \times 7 =$

(18) $8 \times 2 =$

(19) $8 \times 8 =$

(20) $8 \times 6 =$

21 Multiplication 8

8 × 1 to 8 × 10

■ Multiply.

(1) $8 \times 7 =$

(2) $8 \times 3 =$

(3) $8 \times 6 =$

(4) $8 \times 1 =$

(5) $8 \times 10 =$

(6) $8 \times 5 =$

(7) $8 \times 9 =$

(8) $8 \times 4 =$

(9) $8 \times 2 =$

(10) $8 \times 8 =$

(11) $8 \times 2 =$

(12) $8 \times 5 =$

(13) $8 \times 9 =$

(14) $8 \times 7 =$

(15) $8 \times 3 =$

(16) $8 \times 1 =$

(17) $8 \times 8 =$

(18) $8 \times 6 =$

(19) $8 \times 4 =$

(20) $8 \times 10 =$

■ Multiply.

(1) $8 \times 1 =$

(2) $8 \times 8 =$

(3) $8 \times 10 =$

(4) $8 \times 3 =$

(5) $8 \times 6 =$

(6) $8 \times 2 =$

(7) $8 \times 7 =$

(8) $8 \times 4 =$

(9) $8 \times 5 =$

(10) $8 \times 9 =$

(11) $8 \times 4 =$

(12) $8 \times 9 =$

(13) $8 \times 1 =$

(14) $8 \times 5 =$

(15) $8 \times 10 =$

(16) $8 \times 6 =$

(17) $8 \times 2 =$

(18) $8 \times 8 =$

(19) $8 \times 3 =$

(20) $8 \times 7 =$

Review
Multiplication 6, 7, 8

To parents/guardians: After your child finishes one sheet, please check the answers. If your child seems to have made a mistake in the answer, ask them to think again. If your child gets all the answers correct, please offer lots of praise.

■ Multiply.

(1) $6 \times 1 =$

(2) $6 \times 2 =$

(3) $6 \times 3 =$

(4) $7 \times 4 =$

(5) $7 \times 5 =$

(6) $7 \times 6 =$

(7) $8 \times 7 =$

(8) $8 \times 8 =$

(9) $8 \times 9 =$

(10) $8 \times 10 =$

(11) $6 \times 10 =$

(12) $7 \times 3 =$

(13) $8 \times 4 =$

(14) $6 \times 9 =$

(15) $7 \times 2 =$

(16) $8 \times 1 =$

(17) $6 \times 7 =$

(18) $7 \times 8 =$

(19) $8 \times 2 =$

(20) $8 \times 5 =$

■ Multiply.

(1) $6 \times 9 =$

(2) $7 \times 7 =$

(3) $8 \times 5 =$

(4) $8 \times 6 =$

(5) $6 \times 1 =$

(6) $7 \times 8 =$

(7) $8 \times 10 =$

(8) $7 \times 3 =$

(9) $6 \times 2 =$

(10) $8 \times 4 =$

(11) $7 \times 10 =$

(12) $6 \times 3 =$

(13) $8 \times 1 =$

(14) $6 \times 8 =$

(15) $7 \times 5 =$

(16) $6 \times 6 =$

(17) $8 \times 2 =$

(18) $7 \times 4 =$

(19) $8 \times 9 =$

(20) $6 \times 7 =$

23 Practicing Numbers
9 – 90

Name

Date

/ /

To parents/guardians: You may want to encourage your child to repeat the number that increases by 9 while looking at a number chart or addition problem.

■ Draw a line from 9 to 90 in order while saying each number aloud.

■ Say each number aloud as you trace it.

| 9 | 18 | 27 | 36 | 45 | 54 | 63 | 72 | 81 | 90 |

■ Add.

(1) $9 + 9 = 18$

(2) $9 + 9 + 9 = 27$

(3) $9 + 9 + 9 + 9 = 36$

(4) $9 + 9 + 9 + 9 + 9 = 45$

(5) $9 + 9 + 9 + 9 + 9 + 9 = 54$

(6) $9 + 9 + 9 + 9 + 9 + 9 + 9 = 63$

(7) $9 + 9 + 9 + 9 + 9 + 9 + 9 + 9 = 72$

(8) $9 + 9 + 9 + 9 + 9 + 9 + 9 + 9 + 9 = 81$

(9) $9 + 9 + 9 + 9 + 9 + 9 + 9 + 9 + 9 + 9 = 90$

■ Say each number aloud as you trace it.

9	18	27	36	45	54	63	72	81	90

■ Say each number aloud as you trace it.

9	18	27	36	45

(1) $9 + 9 = 18$

(2) $9 + 9 + 9 = 27$

(3) $9 + 9 + 9 + 9 = 36$

(4) $9 + 9 + 9 + 9 + 9 = 45$

■ Write the numbers on the number line. Then add the numbers below.

9				

(1) $9 + 9 =$

(2) $9 + 9 + 9 =$

(3) $9 + 9 + 9 + 9 =$

(4) $9 + 9 + 9 + 9 + 9 =$

■ Say each number aloud as you trace it.

54	63	72	81	90

(1) $9 + 9 + 9 + 9 + 9 + 9 = 54$

(2) $9 + 9 + 9 + 9 + 9 + 9 + 9 = 63$

(3) $9 + 9 + 9 + 9 + 9 + 9 + 9 + 9 = 72$

(4) $9 + 9 + 9 + 9 + 9 + 9 + 9 + 9 + 9 = 81$

(5) $9 + 9 + 9 + 9 + 9 + 9 + 9 + 9 + 9 + 9 = 90$

■ Write the numbers on the number line. Then add the numbers below.

54			

(1) $9 + 9 + 9 + 9 + 9 + 9 =$

(2) $9 + 9 + 9 + 9 + 9 + 9 + 9 =$

(3) $9 + 9 + 9 + 9 + 9 + 9 + 9 + 9 =$

(4) $9 + 9 + 9 + 9 + 9 + 9 + 9 + 9 + 9 =$

(5) $9 + 9 + 9 + 9 + 9 + 9 + 9 + 9 + 9 + 9 =$

Multiplication 9
9 × 1 to 9 × 10

To parents/guardians: Starting on this page, your child will practice the multiplication table for the number 9. Give your child lots of praise when they can read each number sentence well.

■ Read the multiplication table aloud.

Multiplication Table						
(1)	9	×	1	=	9	**Nine times one is nine.**
(2)	9	×	2	=	18	**Nine times two is eighteen.**
(3)	9	×	3	=	27	**Nine times three is twenty-seven.**
(4)	9	×	4	=	36	**Nine times four is thirty-six.**
(5)	9	×	5	=	45	**Nine times five is forty-five.**
(6)	9	×	6	=	54	**Nine times six is fifty-four.**
(7)	9	×	7	=	63	**Nine times seven is sixty-three.**
(8)	9	×	8	=	72	**Nine times eight is seventy-two.**
(9)	9	×	9	=	81	**Nine times nine is eighty-one.**
(10)	9	×	10	=	90	**Nine times ten is ninety.**

■ Read each number sentence aloud as you trace the answer.

(1) 9 × 1 = 9   (6) 9 × 6 = 54

(2) 9 × 2 = 18   (7) 9 × 7 = 63

(3) 9 × 3 = 27   (8) 9 × 8 = 72

(4) 9 × 4 = 36   (9) 9 × 9 = 81

(5) 9 × 5 = 45   (10) 9 × 10 = 90

■Multiply.

(1) 9 × 1 =

(2) 9 × 2 =

(3) 9 × 3 =

(4) 9 × 4 =

(5) 9 × 5 =

(6) 9 × 6 =

(7) 9 × 7 =

(8) 9 × 8 =

(9) 9 × 9 =

(10) 9 × 10 =

(11) 9 × 1 =

(12) 9 × 2 =

(13) 9 × 3 =

(14) 9 × 4 =

(15) 9 × 5 =

(16) 9 × 6 =

(17) 9 × 7 =

(18) 9 × 8 =

(19) 9 × 9 =

(20) 9 × 10 =

26 Multiplication 9
9×1 to 9×10

Name

Date
/ /

To parents/guardians: If your child has difficulty with the problems on this page, you can have them review the Multiplication Table on the previous page for help.

■ Multiply.

(1) $9 \times 3 =$

(2) $9 \times 6 =$

(3) $9 \times 9 =$

(4) $9 \times 5 =$

(5) $9 \times 1 =$

(6) $9 \times 7 =$

(7) $9 \times 2 =$

(8) $9 \times 8 =$

(9) $9 \times 10 =$

(10) $9 \times 4 =$

(11) $9 \times 9 =$

(12) $9 \times 1 =$

(13) $9 \times 7 =$

(14) $9 \times 10 =$

(15) $9 \times 8 =$

(16) $9 \times 3 =$

(17) $9 \times 5 =$

(18) $9 \times 2 =$

(19) $9 \times 4 =$

(20) $9 \times 6 =$

■ Multiply.

(1) $9 \times 7 =$

(2) $9 \times 4 =$

(3) $9 \times 10 =$

(4) $9 \times 2 =$

(5) $9 \times 6 =$

(6) $9 \times 1 =$

(7) $9 \times 8 =$

(8) $9 \times 3 =$

(9) $9 \times 9 =$

(10) $9 \times 5 =$

(11) $9 \times 9 =$

(12) $9 \times 3 =$

(13) $9 \times 1 =$

(14) $9 \times 4 =$

(15) $9 \times 10 =$

(16) $9 \times 5 =$

(17) $9 \times 7 =$

(18) $9 \times 2 =$

(19) $9 \times 8 =$

(20) $9 \times 6 =$

27 Multiplication 9

9×1 to 9×10

■ Multiply.

(1) $9 \times 7 =$

(11) $9 \times 2 =$

(2) $9 \times 3 =$

(12) $9 \times 5 =$

(3) $9 \times 6 =$

(13) $9 \times 9 =$

(4) $9 \times 1 =$

(14) $9 \times 7 =$

(5) $9 \times 10 =$

(15) $9 \times 3 =$

(6) $9 \times 5 =$

(16) $9 \times 1 =$

(7) $9 \times 9 =$

(17) $9 \times 8 =$

(8) $9 \times 4 =$

(18) $9 \times 6 =$

(9) $9 \times 2 =$

(19) $9 \times 4 =$

(10) $9 \times 8 =$

(20) $9 \times 10 =$

■ Multiply.

(1) $9 \times 1 =$

(2) $9 \times 8 =$

(3) $9 \times 10 =$

(4) $9 \times 3 =$

(5) $9 \times 6 =$

(6) $9 \times 2 =$

(7) $9 \times 7 =$

(8) $9 \times 4 =$

(9) $9 \times 5 =$

(10) $9 \times 9 =$

(11) $9 \times 4 =$

(12) $9 \times 9 =$

(13) $9 \times 1 =$

(14) $9 \times 5 =$

(15) $9 \times 10 =$

(16) $9 \times 6 =$

(17) $9 \times 2 =$

(18) $9 \times 8 =$

(19) $9 \times 3 =$

(20) $9 \times 7 =$

Review
Multiplication 7, 8, 9

To parents/guardians: Please confirm your child is able to write the correct answer. If your child answers the multiplication problems correctly, offer lots of praise.

■ Multiply.

(1) 7 × 1 =

(2) 7 × 2 =

(3) 7 × 3 =

(4) 8 × 4 =

(5) 8 × 5 =

(6) 8 × 6 =

(7) 9 × 7 =

(8) 9 × 8 =

(9) 9 × 9 =

(10) 9 × 10 =

(11) 7 × 10 =

(12) 8 × 3 =

(13) 9 × 4 =

(14) 7 × 9 =

(15) 8 × 5 =

(16) 9 × 1 =

(17) 7 × 7 =

(18) 8 × 6 =

(19) 9 × 2 =

(20) 9 × 9 =

■Multiply.

(1) $7 \times 9 =$

(2) $8 \times 7 =$

(3) $9 \times 5 =$

(4) $9 \times 6 =$

(5) $7 \times 1 =$

(6) $8 \times 8 =$

(7) $9 \times 10 =$

(8) $8 \times 3 =$

(9) $7 \times 2 =$

(10) $9 \times 4 =$

(11) $8 \times 10 =$

(12) $7 \times 3 =$

(13) $9 \times 1 =$

(14) $7 \times 8 =$

(15) $8 \times 5 =$

(16) $7 \times 6 =$

(17) $9 \times 2 =$

(18) $8 \times 4 =$

(19) $9 \times 9 =$

(20) $7 \times 7 =$

29 Practicing Numbers
10−100

Name

Date
/ /

To parents/guardians: You may want to encourage your child to repeat the number that increases by 10 while looking at a number chart or addition problem.

■ Draw a line from 10 to 100 in order while saying each number aloud.

■ Say each number aloud as you trace it.

| 10 | 20 | 30 | 40 | 50 | 60 | 70 | 80 | 90 | 100 |

■ Add.

(1) $10+10= 20$

(2) $10+10+10= 30$

(3) $10+10+10+10= 40$

(4) $10+10+10+10+10= 50$

(5) $10+10+10+10+10+10= 60$

(6) $10+10+10+10+10+10+10= 70$

(7) $10+10+10+10+10+10+10+10= 80$

(8) $10+10+10+10+10+10+10+10+10= 90$

(9) $10+10+10+10+10+10+10+10+10+10= 100$

■ Say each number aloud as you trace it.

10	20	30	40	50	60	70	80	90	100

30 Practicing Repeated Addition

10 – 100

■ Say each number aloud as you trace it.

10	20	30	40	50

(1) $10+10= 20$

(2) $10+10+10= 30$

(3) $10+10+10+10= 40$

(4) $10+10+10+10+10= 50$

■ Write the numbers on the number line. Then add the numbers below.

10			

(1) $10+10=$

(2) $10+10+10=$

(3) $10+10+10+10=$

(4) $10+10+10+10+10=$

■ Say each number aloud as you trace it.

60	70	80	90	100

(1) $10+10+10+10+10+10 = 60$

(2) $10+10+10+10+10+10+10 = 70$

(3) $10+10+10+10+10+10+10+10 = 80$

(4) $10+10+10+10+10+10+10+10+10 = 90$

(5) $10+10+10+10+10+10+10+10+10+10 = 100$

■ Write the numbers on the number line. Then add the numbers below.

60			

(1) $10+10+10+10+10+10 =$

(2) $10+10+10+10+10+10+10 =$

(3) $10+10+10+10+10+10+10+10 =$

(4) $10+10+10+10+10+10+10+10+10 =$

(5) $10+10+10+10+10+10+10+10+10+10 =$

Multiplication 10
10×1 to 10×10

To parents/guardians: Starting on this page, your child will practice the multiplication table for the number 10. If your child has difficulty understanding these number sentences, help them understand that 10 × 3 is "three groups of ten."

■ Read the multiplication table aloud.

Multiplication Table

(1)	10 × 1 = 10	Ten times one is ten.
(2)	10 × 2 = 20	Ten times two is twenty.
(3)	10 × 3 = 30	Ten times three is thirty.
(4)	10 × 4 = 40	Ten times four is forty.
(5)	10 × 5 = 50	Ten times five is fifty.
(6)	10 × 6 = 60	Ten times six is sixty.
(7)	10 × 7 = 70	Ten times seven is seventy.
(8)	10 × 8 = 80	Ten times eight is eighty.
(9)	10 × 9 = 90	Ten times nine is ninety.
(10)	10 × 10 = 100	Ten times ten is one hundred.

■ Read each number sentence aloud as you trace the answer.

(1) 10 × 1 = 10

(2) 10 × 2 = 20

(3) 10 × 3 = 30

(4) 10 × 4 = 40

(5) 10 × 5 = 50

(6) 10 × 6 = 60

(7) 10 × 7 = 70

(8) 10 × 8 = 80

(9) 10 × 9 = 90

(10) 10 × 10 = 100

■ Multiply.

(1) $10 \times 1 =$

(2) $10 \times 2 =$

(3) $10 \times 3 =$

(4) $10 \times 4 =$

(5) $10 \times 5 =$

(6) $10 \times 6 =$

(7) $10 \times 7 =$

(8) $10 \times 8 =$

(9) $10 \times 9 =$

(10) $10 \times 10 =$

(11) $10 \times 1 =$

(12) $10 \times 2 =$

(13) $10 \times 3 =$

(14) $10 \times 4 =$

(15) $10 \times 5 =$

(16) $10 \times 6 =$

(17) $10 \times 7 =$

(18) $10 \times 8 =$

(19) $10 \times 9 =$

(20) $10 \times 10 =$

32 Multiplication 10

10 × 1 to 10 × 10

To parents/guardians: If answering the multiplication problems is difficult for your child, they can go back to the previous unit and look at the Multiplication Table. It is a good idea to read the Multiplication Table repeatedly.

■ Multiply.

(1) 10 × 3 =

(2) 10 × 6 =

(3) 10 × 9 =

(4) 10 × 5 =

(5) 10 × 1 =

(6) 10 × 7 =

(7) 10 × 2 =

(8) 10 × 8 =

(9) 10 × 10 =

(10) 10 × 4 =

(11) 10 × 9 =

(12) 10 × 1 =

(13) 10 × 7 =

(14) 10 × 10 =

(15) 10 × 8 =

(16) 10 × 3 =

(17) 10 × 5 =

(18) 10 × 2 =

(19) 10 × 4 =

(20) 10 × 6 =

■ Multiply.

(1) $10 \times 4 =$

(2) $10 \times 7 =$

(3) $10 \times 10 =$

(4) $10 \times 2 =$

(5) $10 \times 6 =$

(6) $10 \times 1 =$

(7) $10 \times 8 =$

(8) $10 \times 3 =$

(9) $10 \times 9 =$

(10) $10 \times 5 =$

(11) $10 \times 9 =$

(12) $10 \times 3 =$

(13) $10 \times 1 =$

(14) $10 \times 4 =$

(15) $10 \times 10 =$

(16) $10 \times 5 =$

(17) $10 \times 7 =$

(18) $10 \times 2 =$

(19) $10 \times 8 =$

(20) $10 \times 6 =$

33 Multiplication 10
10 × 1 to 10 × 10

■ Multiply.

(1)　10 × 7 =

(2)　10 × 3 =

(3)　10 × 6 =

(4)　10 × 1 =

(5)　10 × 10 =

(6)　10 × 5 =

(7)　10 × 9 =

(8)　10 × 4 =

(9)　10 × 2 =

(10)　10 × 8 =

(11)　10 × 2 =

(12)　10 × 5 =

(13)　10 × 9 =

(14)　10 × 7 =

(15)　10 × 3 =

(16)　10 × 1 =

(17)　10 × 8 =

(18)　10 × 6 =

(19)　10 × 4 =

(20)　10 × 10 =

■Multiply.

(1) $10 \times 1 =$

(2) $10 \times 8 =$

(3) $10 \times 10 =$

(4) $10 \times 3 =$

(5) $10 \times 6 =$

(6) $10 \times 2 =$

(7) $10 \times 7 =$

(8) $10 \times 4 =$

(9) $10 \times 5 =$

(10) $10 \times 9 =$

(11) $10 \times 4 =$

(12) $10 \times 9 =$

(13) $10 \times 1 =$

(14) $10 \times 5 =$

(15) $10 \times 10 =$

(16) $10 \times 6 =$

(17) $10 \times 2 =$

(18) $10 \times 8 =$

(19) $10 \times 3 =$

(20) $10 \times 7 =$

Name   Date

To parents/guardians: Please confirm your child is able to write the correct answer. If your child answers the multiplication problems correctly, offer lots of praise.

■ Multiply.

(1) $8 \times 1 =$

(2) $8 \times 2 =$

(3) $8 \times 3 =$

(4) $9 \times 4 =$

(5) $9 \times 5 =$

(6) $9 \times 6 =$

(7) $10 \times 7 =$

(8) $10 \times 8 =$

(9) $10 \times 9 =$

(10) $10 \times 10 =$

(11) $8 \times 10 =$

(12) $9 \times 3 =$

(13) $10 \times 4 =$

(14) $8 \times 9 =$

(15) $9 \times 2 =$

(16) $10 \times 1 =$

(17) $8 \times 7 =$

(18) $9 \times 9 =$

(19) $10 \times 2 =$

(20) $10 \times 6 =$

■ Multiply.

(1) $8 \times 9 =$

(2) $9 \times 7 =$

(3) $10 \times 5 =$

(4) $10 \times 6 =$

(5) $8 \times 1 =$

(6) $9 \times 8 =$

(7) $9 \times 9 =$

(8) $10 \times 3 =$

(9) $8 \times 2 =$

(10) $10 \times 4 =$

(11) $9 \times 10 =$

(12) $8 \times 3 =$

(13) $10 \times 1 =$

(14) $8 \times 8 =$

(15) $9 \times 5 =$

(16) $9 \times 6 =$

(17) $10 \times 2 =$

(18) $9 \times 4 =$

(19) $10 \times 9 =$

(20) $8 \times 7 =$

35 Review
Multiplication 6 – 10

Name

Date   /   /

To parents/guardians: From this page on, your child will review multiplication from 6 to 10. If they have difficulty, please return to previous pages for further practice.

■ Multiply.

(1)　6　×　3　=

(2)　7　×　7　=

(3)　8　×　9　=

(4)　9　×　4　=

(5)　10　×　6　=

(6)　9　×　8　=

(7)　6　×　5　=

(8)　7　×　10　=

(9)　10　×　2　=

(10)　8　×　8　=

(11)　9　×　2　=

(12)　8　×　3　=

(13)　10　×　9　=

(14)　6　×　10　=

(15)　7　×　5　=

(16)　9　×　9　=

(17)　10　×　4　=

(18)　6　×　7　=

(19)　7　×　8　=

(20)　8　×　1　=

■Multiply.

(1) $10 \times 1 =$

(2) $6 \times 2 =$

(3) $7 \times 4 =$

(4) $8 \times 6 =$

(5) $9 \times 10 =$

(6) $6 \times 6 =$

(7) $7 \times 8 =$

(8) $8 \times 7 =$

(9) $9 \times 3 =$

(10) $10 \times 4 =$

(11) $7 \times 10 =$

(12) $8 \times 2 =$

(13) $9 \times 1 =$

(14) $10 \times 8 =$

(15) $6 \times 5 =$

(16) $8 \times 4 =$

(17) $9 \times 2 =$

(18) $10 \times 3 =$

(19) $6 \times 9 =$

(20) $7 \times 7 =$

36 Review
Multiplication 6 – 10

■ Multiply.

(1) $9 \times 2 =$

(2) $6 \times 7 =$

(3) $8 \times 9 =$

(4) $10 \times 4 =$

(5) $7 \times 6 =$

(6) $8 \times 10 =$

(7) $6 \times 1 =$

(8) $9 \times 7 =$

(9) $7 \times 2 =$

(10) $10 \times 5 =$

(11) $10 \times 2 =$

(12) $7 \times 3 =$

(13) $9 \times 9 =$

(14) $6 \times 10 =$

(15) $8 \times 5 =$

(16) $7 \times 9 =$

(17) $6 \times 4 =$

(18) $10 \times 7 =$

(19) $7 \times 8 =$

(20) $8 \times 1 =$

■ Multiply.

(1)　6 × 4 =

(2)　8 × 2 =

(3)　10 × 9 =

(4)　7 × 6 =

(5)　9 × 10 =

(6)　7 × 1 =

(7)　10 × 8 =

(8)　8 × 7 =

(9)　6 × 3 =

(10)　9 × 5 =

(11)　10 × 10 =

(12)　8 × 3 =

(13)　9 × 1 =

(14)　6 × 8 =

(15)　7 × 5 =

(16)　8 × 6 =

(17)　6 × 2 =

(18)　9 × 4 =

(19)　7 × 9 =

(20)　10 × 7 =

Review
Multiplication 1 – 10

■ Multiply.

(1) $1 \times 5 =$

(2) $1 \times 10 =$

(3) $2 \times 4 =$

(4) $2 \times 8 =$

(5) $3 \times 6 =$

(6) $3 \times 2 =$

(7) $4 \times 9 =$

(8) $4 \times 1 =$

(9) $5 \times 3 =$

(10) $5 \times 7 =$

(11) $6 \times 3 =$

(12) $6 \times 9 =$

(13) $7 \times 2 =$

(14) $7 \times 4 =$

(15) $8 \times 1 =$

(16) $8 \times 8 =$

(17) $9 \times 5 =$

(18) $9 \times 7 =$

(19) $10 \times 6 =$

(20) $10 \times 10 =$

■ Multiply.

(1) $1 \times 3 =$

(2) $2 \times 5 =$

(3) $3 \times 8 =$

(4) $4 \times 10 =$

(5) $5 \times 6 =$

(6) $6 \times 1 =$

(7) $7 \times 7 =$

(8) $8 \times 4 =$

(9) $9 \times 2 =$

(10) $10 \times 9 =$

(11) $1 \times 9 =$

(12) $2 \times 6 =$

(13) $3 \times 4 =$

(14) $4 \times 5 =$

(15) $5 \times 8 =$

(16) $6 \times 7 =$

(17) $7 \times 1 =$

(18) $8 \times 10 =$

(19) $9 \times 3 =$

(20) $10 \times 2 =$

38 Review
Multiplication 1 – 10

■ Multiply.

(1) $4 \times 3 =$ (11) $2 \times 7 =$

(2) $8 \times 2 =$ (12) $6 \times 1 =$

(3) $7 \times 1 =$ (13) $3 \times 9 =$

(4) $10 \times 8 =$ (14) $4 \times 5 =$

(5) $5 \times 9 =$ (15) $10 \times 2 =$

(6) $6 \times 7 =$ (16) $1 \times 8 =$

(7) $1 \times 4 =$ (17) $9 \times 4 =$

(8) $2 \times 6 =$ (18) $5 \times 6 =$

(9) $3 \times 5 =$ (19) $7 \times 10 =$

(10) $9 \times 10 =$ (20) $8 \times 3 =$

■Multiply.

(1) $9 \times 3 =$

(2) $8 \times 5 =$

(3) $5 \times 8 =$

(4) $3 \times 10 =$

(5) $2 \times 6 =$

(6) $1 \times 1 =$

(7) $4 \times 7 =$

(8) $10 \times 4 =$

(9) $6 \times 2 =$

(10) $7 \times 9 =$

(11) $1 \times 2 =$

(12) $10 \times 3 =$

(13) $7 \times 8 =$

(14) $4 \times 9 =$

(15) $8 \times 6 =$

(16) $5 \times 1 =$

(17) $3 \times 7 =$

(18) $2 \times 10 =$

(19) $9 \times 4 =$

(20) $6 \times 5 =$

Name

Date
/ /

To parents/guardians: When your child has finished this book, give them the Certificate of Achievement found on the final page. Multiplication is a difficult skill to master. Make sure to congratulate your child for completing this workbook!

■ Multiply.

(1) 7 × 9 =

(2) 6 × 5 =

(3) 4 × 8 =

(4) 2 × 7 =

(5) 7 × 8 =

(6) 5 × 1 =

(7) 9 × 4 =

(8) 3 × 9 =

(9) 5 × 4 =

(10) 2 × 2 =

(11) 1 × 7 =

(12) 9 × 3 =

(13) 7 × 6 =

(14) 4 × 5 =

(15) 9 × 9 =

(16) 2 × 6 =

(17) 10 × 9 =

(18) 5 × 6 =

(19) 8 × 5 =

(20) 6 × 8 =

■ Multiply.

(1) $7 \times 3 =$

(2) $8 \times 4 =$

(3) $9 \times 8 =$

(4) $5 \times 8 =$

(5) $10 \times 7 =$

(6) $2 \times 4 =$

(7) $3 \times 9 =$

(8) $6 \times 8 =$

(9) $7 \times 7 =$

(10) $4 \times 3 =$

(11) $9 \times 6 =$

(12) $7 \times 9 =$

(13) $8 \times 8 =$

(14) $5 \times 4 =$

(15) $6 \times 6 =$

(16) $7 \times 2 =$

(17) $4 \times 9 =$

(18) $9 \times 9 =$

(19) $3 \times 8 =$

(20) $10 \times 10 =$

Certificate of Achievement

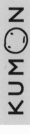

is hereby congratulated on completing

My Book of Multiplication

Presented on   , 20

Parent or Guardian

KUM◯N